BRING ME SUNSHINE	6
BUSY DOING NOTHING	8
CHITTY CHITTY BANG BANG	10
EVERYTHING IS BEAUTIFUL	12
LILY THE PINK	7
NELLIE THE ELEPHANT	14
OVER THE RAINBOW	16
PALOMA BLANCA	18
PUFF (THE MAGIC DRAGON)	20
THE RUNAWAY TRAIN	22
SING	24
SINGIN' IN THE RAIN	23
SPREAD A LITTLE HAPPINESS	26
THE SUN HAS GOT HIS HAT ON	28
SWINGING ON A STAR	30
TALK TO THE ANIMALS	32
THE UMBRELLA MAN	34
WHEN YOU WISH UPON A STAR	40
WOULDN'T IT BE LOVELY	36
Y VIVA ESPANA	38

Edited by PETER FOSS
Arranged by GARY LERNER

Cover design by Graphic Edge
Photographs by Eirik Hevroy Berg
Richmond College

First Published 1989
© International Music Publications

Exclusive Distributors
International Music Publications
Southend Road, Woodford Green,
Essex IG8 8HN, England.

Photocopying of this copyright material is illegal.

215-2-544

FINGERING CHART
Recorder

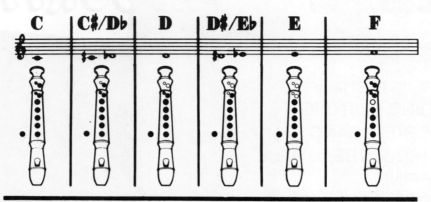

CHORD DIRECTORY
Guitar

'x' over a string means this string should not be played

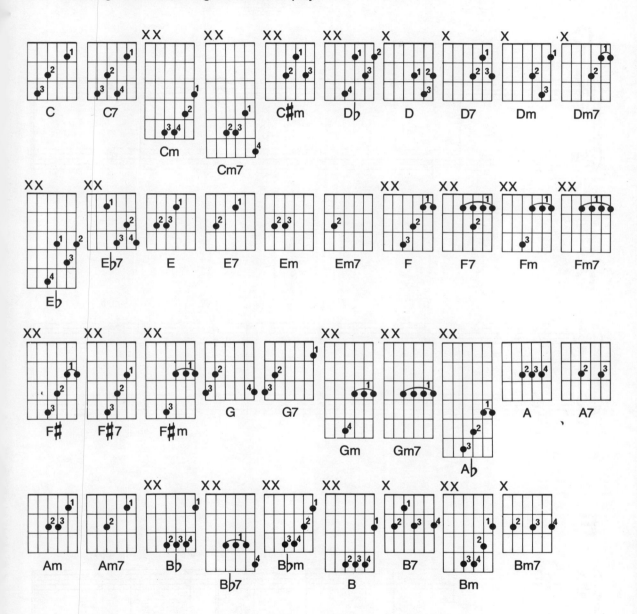

Always make sure your guitar is in tune with the other instruments before you start to play with other musicians.

CHORD SYMBOL GUIDE
Keyboards

C
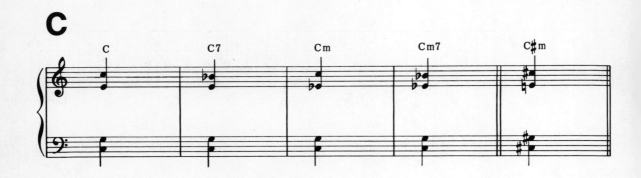

D

E

BRING ME SUNSHINE

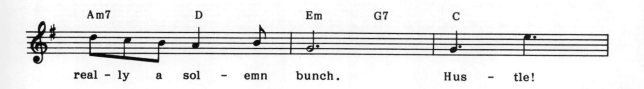

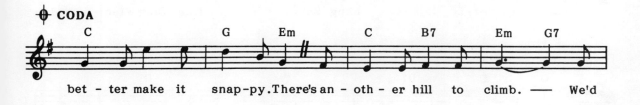

CHITTY CHITTY BANG BANG

Words and Music by
RICHARD M SHERMAN and ROBERT B SHERMAN

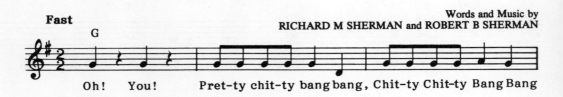

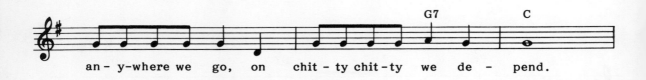
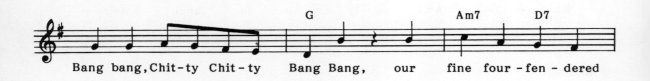

© 1968 & 1989 Unart Music Corp, USA
International Copyright Secured
Used by Permission

EVERYTHING IS BEAUTIFUL

Words and Music
by RAY STEVENS

NELLIE THE ELEPHANT

Words and Music by
RALPH BUTLER and PETER HART

© 1956 & 1989 Dash Music Co Ltd, 8/9 Frith Street, London W1V 5TZ

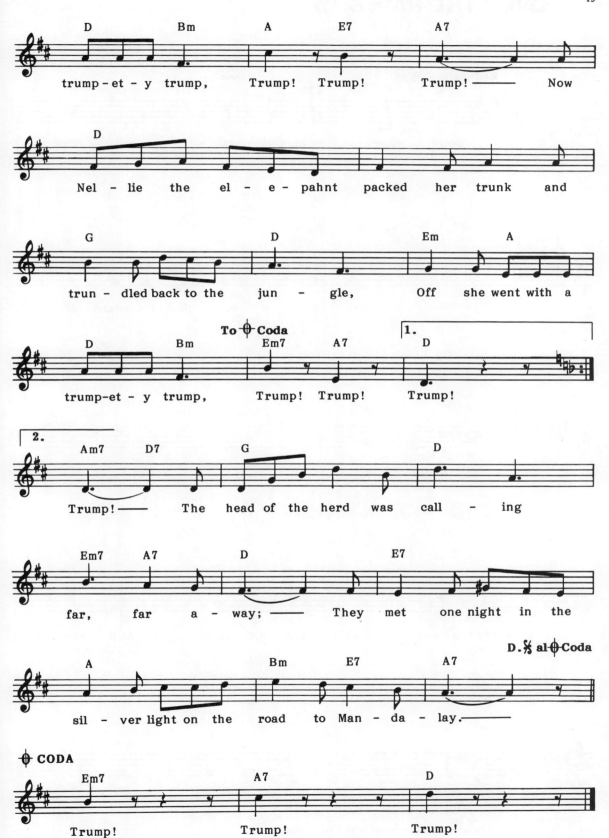

OVER THE RAINBOW

Words by E Y HARBURG
Music by HAROLD ARLEN

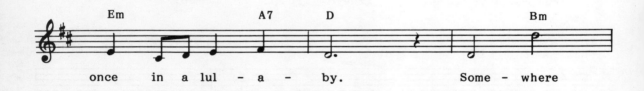
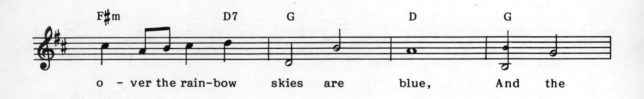
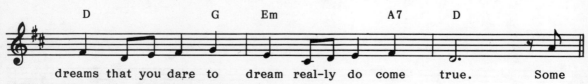

© 1938, 1939, 1966, 1967 & 1989 Metro-Goldwin-Mayer Inc
All rights controlled by Leo Feist Inc
Assigned to SBK Catalogue Partnership and administered by SBK Feist Catalog
International Copyright Secured
Used by Permission

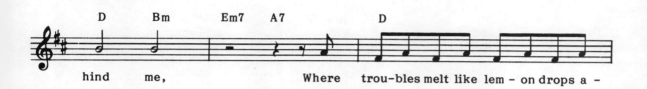
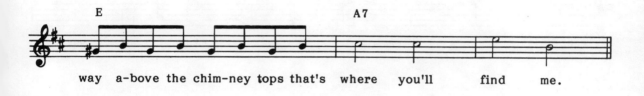

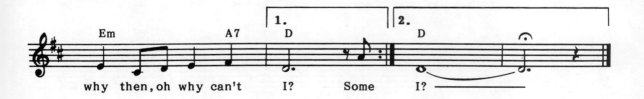

PUFF (The Magic Dragon)

Words and Music by
PETER YARROW and LEONARD LIPTON

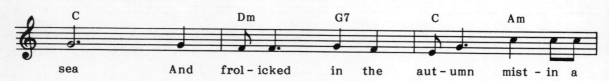

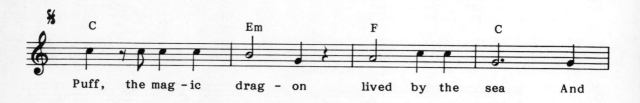

© 1962 & 1989 Pepamar Music Corp, USA
Warner Chappell Music Ltd, London W1Y 3FA

START BUSKING!
Index to Songs

title	book
AGADOO	**HITS OF THE EIGHTIES**
ALEXANDER'S RAGTIME BAND	**JAZZ 'N' BLUES**
'ALLO 'ALLO	**NEIGHBOURS AND OTHER TV THEMES**
ALWAYS ON MY MIND	**HITS OF THE EIGHTIES**
ARTHUR'S THEME (BEST THAT YOU CAN DO)	**HITS OF THE EIGHTIES**
BAKER STREET	**VIDEO SPECTACULAR**
BEN	**HITS OF THE EIGHTIES**
BILL BAILEY WON'T YOU PLEASE COME HOME	**JAZZ 'N' BLUES**
BIRTH OF THE BLUES, THE	**JAZZ 'N' BLUES**
BLACK BOTTOM	**JAZZ 'N' BLUES**
BOY FROM NOWHERE	**HITS OF THE EIGHTIES**
BRING ME SUNSHINE	**EASY FAVOURITES**
BUSY DOING NOTHING	**EASY FAVOURITES**
CARAVAN OF LOVE	**VIDEO SPECTACULAR**
CARELESS WHISPER	**VIDEO SPECTACULAR**
CHARLESTON	**JAZZ 'N' BLUES**
CHEROKEE	**JAZZ 'N' BLUES**
CHICAGO	**JAZZ 'N' BLUES**
CHINA IN YOUR HAND	**HITS OF THE EIGHTIES**
CHITTY CHITTY BANG BANG	**EASY FAVOURITES**
COMING AROUND AGAIN	**HITS OF THE EIGHTIES**
CORONATION STREET	**NEIGHBOURS AND OTHER TV THEMES**
CRAZY RHYTHM	**JAZZ 'N' BLUES**
DANCING IN THE STREET	**CHART SENSATIONS**
DARKTOWN STRUTTERS BALL, THE	**JAZZ 'N' BLUES**
DON'T GO BREAKING MY HEART	**CHART SENSATIONS**
EASTENDERS	**NEIGHBOURS AND OTHER TV THEMES**
ENTERTAINER, THE	**JAZZ 'N' BLUES**
EVERY BREATH YOU TAKE	**CHART SENSATIONS**
EVERY TIME YOU GO AWAY	**HITS OF THE EIGHTIES**
EVERYTHING I OWN	**CHART SENSATIONS**
EVRYTHING IS BEAUTIFUL	**EASY FAVOURITES**
EYE OF THE TIGER	**VIDEO SPECTACULAR**
FAME	**NEIGHBOURS AND OTHER TV THEMES**
FAWLTY TOWERS	**NEIGHBOURS AND OTHER TV THEMES**
FLASHDANCE...WHAT A FEELING	**HITS OF THE EIGHTIES**

title	book
FREEDOM	**VIDEO SPECTACULAR**
GREATEST LOVE OF ALL, THE	**VIDEO SPECTACULAR**
GROOVY KIND OF LOVE	**CHART SENSATIONS**
HE'S GOT THE WHOLE WORLD IN HIS HANDS	**JAZZ 'N' BLUES**
HEAVEN — HIGHWAY TO HEAVEN	**NEIGHBOURS AND OTHER TV THEMES**
HELLO	**CHART SENSATIONS**
HILL STREET BLUES	**NEIGHBOURS AND OTHER TV THEMES**
I COULD BE SO GOOD FOR YOU — MINDER	**NEIGHBOURS AND OTHER TV THEMES**
I GOT RHYTHM	**JAZZ 'N' BLUES**
I JUST CALLED TO SAY I LOVE YOU	**CHART SENSATIONS**
I JUST CAN'T STOP LOVING YOU	**VIDEO SPECTACULAR**
I WANT TO KNOW WHAT LOVE IS	**CHART SENSATIONS**
I WISH I KNEW HOW IT WOULD FEEL TO BE FREE — FILM 89	**NEIGHBOURS AND OTHER TV THEMES**
I'M GONNA SIT RIGHT DOWN AND WRITE MYSELF A LETTER	**JAZZ 'N' BLUES**
IMAGINE	**CHART SENSATIONS**
IN THE MOOD	**JAZZ 'N' BLUES**
IN YOUR EYES	**VIDEO SPECTACULAR**
INTO THE GROOVE	**CHART SENSATIONS**
IT DOESN'T MATTER ANY MORE	**CHART SENSATIONS**
IT'S MY TURN	**HITS OF THE EIGHTIES**
KARMA CHAMELEON	**CHART SENSATIONS**
LA BAMBA	**VIDEO SPECTACULAR**
LA ISLA BONITA	**VIDEO SPECTACULAR**
LAST OF THE SUMMER WINE	**NEIGHBOURS AND OTHER TV THEMES**
LEAN ON ME	**VIDEO SPECTACULAR**
LILY THE PINK	**EASY FAVOURITES**
LIMEHOUSE BLUES	**JAZZ 'N' BLUES**
LITTLE LIES	**HITS OF THE EIGHTIES**
LOCO-MOTION, THE	**CHART SENSATIONS**
LOVE IS LIKE A BUTTERFLY — BUTTERFLIES	**NEIGHBOURS AND OTHER TV THEMES**
LOVE LETTERS	**HITS OF THE EIGHTIES**
LOVE ON THE ROCKS	**HITS OF THE EIGHTIES**
LOVELY DAY	**VIDEO SPECTACULAR**
MATCH OF THE DAY	**NEIGHBOURS AND OTHER TV THEMES**
MISS MARPLE	**NEIGHBOURS AND OTHER TV THEMES**
NEIGHBOURS	**NEIGHBOURS AND OTHER TV THEMES**
NELLIE THE ELEPHANT	**EASY FAVOURITES**
NEVER GONNA GIVE YOU UP	**VIDEO SPECTACULAR**
NIKITA	**HITS OF THE EIGHTIES**
NOTHING'S GONNA STOP US NOW	**CHART SENSATIONS**
ONE DAY IN YOUR LIFE	**CHART SENSATIONS**
ONE MOMENT IN TIME — 1988 OLYMPIC GAMES SONGS	**NEIGHBOURS AND OTHER TV THEMES**

START BUSKING! is a series of six new books — each containing twenty top tunes: songs with lyrics, including chart hits from over the past thirty years as well as hits of the eighties; themes from television's most popular shows and series; jazz standards, and pops from the world of video.

Play START BUSKING! on — C INSTRUMENTS (treble clef)
— GUITAR
— KEYBOARDS

EASY FAVOURITES
Nellie the elephant
and many other friendly faces.
Order ref: 17056

JAZZ 'N BLUES
Have a great time at the
Dark Town Strutter's Ball.
Order ref: 17053

'NEIGHBOURS' & OTHER TV THEMES
Telly addict or not you'll know all these top tunes.
Order ref: 17055

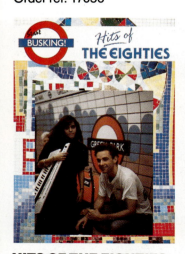

HITS OF THE EIGHTIES
. . . soon to become the classics of the future.
Order ref: 17058

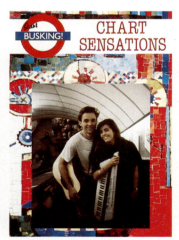

CHART SENSATIONS
A package of chartbusters selected from thirty years of No.1 hits.
Order ref: 17057

VIDEO SPECTACULAR
Big hits from today's headlining groups and personalities.
Order ref: 17054

What is busking?

Everyone has seen and heard street musicians playing — usually for money — in busy shopping centres, tube stations, and wherever people regularly pass by. Some musicians play 'serious' music, each performer reading from a part. Perhaps more often, however, the music consists of pop songs and well-known tunes. These are usually played from memory and the songs are often performed solo by a singer-guitarist.

In these situations, the performers are almost sure to do one thing: interpret the music in their own way, adding rhythmic twists and turns and occasionally adapting the tune to suit their own instrument, playing style, or mood of the moment. Sometimes the melody may be only half-remembered at the outset, and the musician may even have to make some of it up! This very individual and casual approach to playing and performing music is called *busking*.

In this series of books, you — the busker — are provided with the tune, and from then on it's up to you!

What START BUSKING! offers the young player

1. Each tune has been adapted and arranged specifically with inexperienced players in mind:

    — Difficult rhythms have, where possible, been simplified without losing the 'feel' of the music.

    — Only very basic chord symbols have been used.

    — All the tunes are in easy keys, transpositions having been made where necessary.

    — The tunes, although primarily pitched for recorder (notes too high or too low have cued alternatives) will adapt easily for all treble clef instruments.

2. Each book in the series contains three instrumental guides:

    — GUITARISTS: an easy-to-read *Chord Directory* which lists all the chords used in the series.

    — KEYBOARD PLAYERS: A *Chord Symbol Guide* with chords written out in full notation.

    — RECORDER PLAYERS: A two-octave *Fingering Chart*.

The Value of START BUSKING! for Teachers and Students of Music

Today, everyone is aware of, and indeed often affected by the music which surrounds us: on television, radio, in the cinema, supermarkets, shopping precincts, etc. And it would be unusual for anyone studying music or an instrument not to want to play at least one or two of these familiar tunes.

It is an accepted educational principle that knowledge gained as the result of a student's own research and personal interest in a subject is more readily absorbed than that acquired through traditional teaching methods. START BUSKING! provides the music student *or anyone interested in music* with a wealth of learning possibilities.

For the keyboard player, busking is an ideal way of developing the essential skill of keyboard harmony: the ability to 'feel' harmonic progressions at the keyboard and to develop these into a convincing improvisation or accompaniment. The chord symbols used in START BUSKING! are deliberately straightforward — only major and minor chords, and chords with the minor seventh are used. But at any time, once the player is familiar with the harmonic sequence of any song, the possibility is open for adding other more adventurous chords to the basic framework. Working out these extra harmonic possibilities — initially most probably by trial and error — will prove a valuable and entertaining experience for any budding musician.

For the 'solo-line' instrumentalist (flute, recorder, violin, etc.) there are other possibilities. When the melody line can be played easily and with musical fluency, the way is open for the performer's own ideas to come to the fore: relaxing the rhythms, or adapting the melody with extra notes, decorative passage work or melodic riffs. Finding out which extra notes will fit and which will not is all part and parcel of the educational experience that can be gained through busking.

Finally, START BUSKING! provides an ideal opportunity for musicians to play together. The six books in the series contain 120 mixed and varied titles; there's something for everyone — to play, learn and most important of all — *enjoy*.

FREE   START BUSKING! — BADGE —
   Pick one up at your Music Shop or write to this address

EDUCATION DIVISION
IMP
International Music Publications
Southend Road, Woodford Green, Essex IG8 8HN, England.

title	book
OVER THE RAINBOW	**EASY FAVOURITES**
PALOMA BLANCA	**EASY FAVOURITES**
PAPA DON'T PREACH	**VIDEO SPECTACULAR**
PUFF (THE MAGIC DRAGON)	**EASY FAVOURITES**
REET PETITE	**VIDEO SPECTACULAR**
RUNAWAY TRAIN, THE	**EASY FAVOURITES**
SAVING ALL MY LOVE FOR YOU	**CHART SENSATIONS**
SAY YOU, SAY ME	**VIDEO SPECTACULAR**
SING	**EASY FAVOURITES**
SINGIN' IN THE RAIN	**EASY FAVOURITES**
SKYLINER	**JAZZ 'N' BLUES**
SPREAD A LITTLE HAPPINESS	**EASY FAVOURITES**
STAND BY ME	**CHART SENSATIONS**
STAND BY YOUR MAN	**CHART SENSATIONS**
STAR TREK	**NEIGHBOURS AND OTHER TV THEMES**
SUMMER HOLIDAY	**CHART SENSATIONS**
SUN HAS GOT HIS HAT ON, THE	**EASY FAVOURITES**
SWEET GEORGIA BROWN	**JAZZ 'N' BLUES**
SWINGING ON A STAR	**EASY FAVOURITES**
TAKE MY BREATH AWAY	**CHART SENSATIONS**
TALK TO THE ANIMALS	**EASY FAVOURITES**
THANK YOU FOR BEING A FRIEND —THE GOLDEN GIRLS	**NEIGHBOURS AND OTHER TV THEMES**
THAT'S LIVING ALRIGHT — AUF WIEDERSEHEN PET	**NEIGHBOURS AND OTHER TV THEMES**
THAT'S WHAT FRIENDS ARE FOR	**HITS OF THE EIGHTIES**
TIGER RAG	**JAZZ 'N' BLUES**
TONIGHT, I CELEBRATE MY LOVE	**HITS OF THE EIGHTIES**
TRUE BLUE	**VIDEO SPECTACULAR**
12TH STREET RAG	**JAZZ 'N' BLUES**
UMBRELLA MAN, THE	**EASY FAVOURITES**
UP WHERE WE BELONG	**HITS OF THE EIGHTIES**
WAKE ME UP BEFORE YOU GO-GO	**VIDEO SPECTACULAR**
WE'VE GOT TONIGHT	**HITS OF THE EIGHTIES**
WHEN THE SAINTS GO MARCHING IN	**JAZZ 'N' BLUES**
WHEN YOU WISH UPON A STAR	**EASY FAVOURITES**
WHO DO YOU THINK YOU ARE KIDDING MR HITLER	**NEIGHBOURS AND OTHER TV THEMES**
WIND BENEATH MY WINGS, THE	**HITS OF THE EIGHTIES**
WOMAN	**HITS OF THE EIGHTIES**
WOMAN IN LOVE	**VIDEO SPECTACULAR**
WOULDN'T IT BE LOVELY	**EASY FAVOURITES**
Y VIVA ESPANA	**EASY FAVOURITES**
YOU WIN AGAIN	**VIDEO SPECTACULAR**

THE RUNAWAY TRAIN

Words by ROBERT E MASSEY
Music by CARSON ROBISON

© 1925 & 1989 Shapiro Bernstein & Co Inc, USA
Sub-published by B Feldman & Co Ltd, London WC2H 0EA

SING

Words and Music by JOE RAPOSO

© 1971, 1974 & 1989 Jonico Music Inc, USA
Assigned to Standard Music Ltd, 1A Farm Place, London W8 7SX
for the territory of the United Kingdom and the Republic of Eire

SPREAD A LITTLE HAPPINESS

Words by CLIFFORD GREY
Music by VIVIAN ELLIS

© 1928 & 1989 Harms Inc, USA
Chappell Music Ltd, London W1Y 3FA

THE SUN HAS GOT HIS HAT ON

SWINGING ON A STAR

Words by JOHNNY BURKE
Music by JIMMY VAN HEUSEN

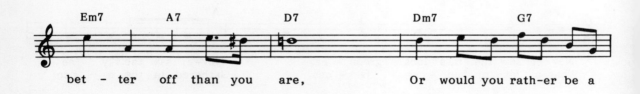

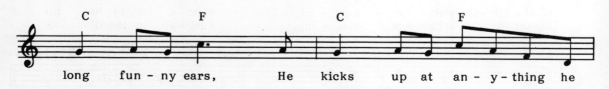

© 1944 & 1989 Burke and Van Heusen Inc, USA
Chappell Morris Ltd, London W1Y 3FA

TALK TO THE ANIMALS

Words and Music by LESLIE BRICUSSE

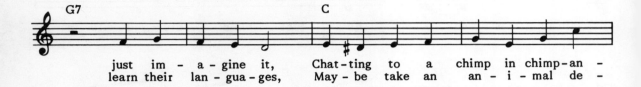

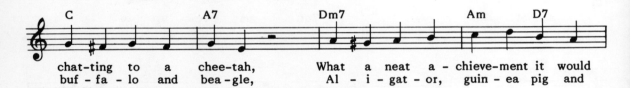

© 1967, 1968 & 1989 Twentieth Century Music Corp, USA
Rights throughout the world controlled by Hastings Music Corp, USA
International Copyright Secured
Used by Permission

THE UMBRELLA MAN

Words by JAMES CAVANAUGH
Music by VINCENT ROSE and LARRY STOCK

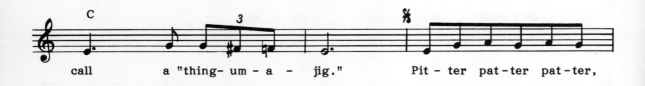

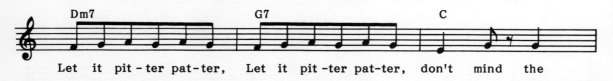

© 1938 & 1989 Harms Inc, USA
Chappell Music Ltd, London W1Y 3FA